Asteroids

Samantha Bonar

Watts LIBRARY

Franklin Watts
A Division of Grolier Publishing
New York • London • Hong Kong • Sydney
Danbury, Connecticut

For my sister, astronomer E. L. Blanton

Note to readers: Definitions for words in **bold** can be found in the Glossary at the back of this book.

Photographs ©: American Museum of Natural History: 38 (126035); AP/Wide World Photos: 45; Corbis-Bettmann: 48 (Livemore National Laboratory, University of California), 20 (UPI); Finley Holiday Film: 17, 18, 19, 28; Lunar Planetary Institute: 34; NASA: 52 (The Johns Hopkins University Applied Physics Laboratory), 23 (R. Kempton/New England Meteoritical Services), 13, 47; National Museum of Natural History, Smithsonian Institution: 3 top, 41; Photo Researchers: 24 (David Nunuk/ SPL), 3 bottom, 16 (Julian Baum/SPL), 6 (John Foster), 37 (Georg Gerster), 7 (Francois Gohier), cover (Roger Harris/SPL), 10, 50 (Science Photo Library), 8, 9 (David Parker/SPL), 4 (D. Van Ravenswaay/SPL), 25 (Wards/SCI/Science Source), 31, 33 (NASA/SPL), 40 (Joe Tucciarone/SPL); Tony Stone Images: 42 (Alan R. Moller).

Solar system diagram created by Greg Harris

Visit Franklin Watts on the Internet at:
http://publishing.grolier.com

Library of Congress Cataloging-in-Publication Data

Bonar, Samantha.
    Asteroids / Samantha Bonar.
       p.   cm.— (Watts Library)
    Includes bibliographical references and index.
    Summary: Describes the location and content of the asteroid belt, the formation and composition of asteroids, and the history of collisions between asteroids and Earth.
    ISBN: 0-531-20367-0 (lib. bdg.)   0-531-16418-7 (pbk.)
    1. Asteroids—Juvenile literature. [1. Asteroids] I. Title. II. Series.
QB651.B56 1999
523.44—dc21
                                   98-25109
                                        CIP
                                        AC

Contents

An artist's idea of what Earth might have looked like about 65 million years ago

Chapter One

Deadly Impact

Life on Earth nearly ended 65 million years ago. If you could travel in a time machine back to that era, you would find yourself in a place with an inky black sky and freezing cold temperatures. When you tried to breathe, you would choke on the thick black dust that filled your eyes, nose, and mouth. The stench of dead and rotting plants and animals would make you sick to your stomach. If you stayed there, you would die.

An artist's representation of an asteroid striking Earth during the Age of the Dinosaurs

Sixty-five million years ago, 70 percent of life on Earth died—including all of the dinosaurs and most of the plants, **reptiles**, **mammals**, and sea creatures. They never knew what hit them. But we know. It was probably an **asteroid**—a rock from outer space.

The Answer to a Puzzling Question

Scientists have known for many years that the dinosaurs were wiped out suddenly. But they didn't know why. In 1980, a geologist named Luis Alvarez suggested that the dinosaurs disappeared because a giant asteroid moving 45,000 miles (72,400 kilometers) per hour smashed into Earth with the force of 100 million nuclear bombs.

The Name Game

When an asteroid is hit by another object in space, it may break into many small pieces. These pieces are called **meteoroids** when they enter Earth's **atmosphere** and **meteorites** when they land on Earth. The glowing light you see when a meteoroid comes into contact with Earth's atmosphere is called a **meteor**.

Some people call meteors shooting stars, but a meteor is not a star. Most meteoroids come from **comets**, not asteroids. Comets are small balls of ice and rock that **orbit** the Sun.

Luis Alvarez based his theory on work done by his son Walter, who was also a geologist. In 1977, while digging deep in the earth in Italy, Walter found a strange layer of 65-million-year-old clay. Teams of scientists led by Walter found the same clay layer at other sites all over the world.

The clay contained huge amounts of **iridium**—a rare metal similar to gold. Iridium is found in only three places: 2,000 miles (3,200 km) underground, in dust that falls to Earth from exploding asteroids and comets, and in meteorites.

Luis Alvarez suggested that the clay was the remains of an asteroid that had originally been 6 to 12 miles (10 to 19 km) wide. The asteroid exploded when it hit Earth, sending 4 trillion tons of iridium-rich dust high into the sky. Some of the dust particles were so small that they stayed in the atmosphere for years, blocking out the Sun's light.

This layer of clay suggests that an asteroid collided with Earth about 65 million years ago.

Luis Alvarez

As you know, plants need sunlight to live. Because the dust blocked out most of the Sun's rays, almost all plants on Earth died. Many dinosaurs and other animals relied on plants for food. When the plants died, so did these creatures. And finally, many of Earth's meat-eaters died.

Alvarez's theory seemed to make sense, but scientists still had one question. If such a huge asteroid hit Earth, it would have left a tremendous crater. Where was that crater?

The Final Piece of Evidence

In 1989, workers drilling for oil on Mexico's Yucatan Peninsula found a 120-mile (190-km)-wide crater about 1 mile (1.6 km) underground. The crater was so large that it extended into the southern part of the Gulf of Mexico. After studying the site in more detail, scientists realized that the crater may have originally been as much as 180 miles (290 km) wide. The crater had most likely been created by an asteroid 6 to 12 miles (10 to 19 km) wide.

In 1992, scientists tested rocks from the crater and determined that the crater was 64.98 million years old. Alvarez had found his impact site. The crater has filled in some since the asteroid hit, but it is still 550 feet (170 meters) deep. Three Statues of Liberty could be laid end to end, and they still wouldn't fill the crater!

In 1996, an even more exciting discovery was made. Scientists found fragments of a 65-million-year-old asteroid off the coast of Florida in the Atlantic Ocean. They think that

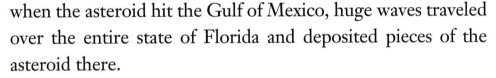

when the asteroid hit the Gulf of Mexico, huge waves traveled over the entire state of Florida and deposited pieces of the asteroid there.

These spherules formed about 65 million years ago when the heat of an asteroid impact melted rocks on Mexico's Yucatan Peninsula.

If the asteroid hadn't hit Earth, the dinosaurs would have continued to dominate the planet. The death of the dinosaurs gave mammals a chance to **evolve**, eventually leading to the development of the human race. The asteroid may be responsible for our very existence.

But another asteroid impact could destroy us. Scientists are working hard to make sure that doesn't happen. Dinosaurs were the dominant land animals on Earth for 140 million years. Humans have been on the planet for less than 1 million. We want to be here a lot longer.

Italian astronomer Giuseppe Piazzi was one of the scientists to look for a planet between Mars and Jupiter.

Chapter Two

The Missing Planet

In the mid-1700s, astronomers were puzzled by a space mystery. When they calculated the distances between the seven planets that they knew about—Mercury, Venus, Earth, Mars, Jupiter, Saturn, and Uranus—they noticed that there was a regular pattern. But one area of space didn't fit the pattern. Based on their positions in space, Jupiter and Mars should have had a planet between them. Where was it?

At a meeting in 1796, astronomers agreed to search the area between Jupiter and Mars for the "missing" planet. On January 1, 1801, an Italian astronomer named Giuseppe Piazzi discovered what he thought was the missing planet. He named the object he observed through his telescope Ceres, after the Greek goddess of the earth.

In 1802, another object was seen between Mars and Jupiter. It was named Pallas, after the Greek goddess of wisdom. In 1804, yet another object was discovered! This one was called Juno, after the queen of the Roman goddesses. Vesta, named after the Roman goddess of the hearth, was spotted in 1807.

The astronomers who had set out to find one planet had instead found four. In the mid-1800s, a German amateur astronomer found fourteen more. By the end of the 1800s, hundreds of objects had been discovered between Jupiter and Mars.

The Asteroid Belt

The objects were given the name *asteroids*, which means "starlike." Asteroids are also called "minor planets." More than 7,000 asteroids have now been discovered, and hundreds more are spotted each year. There are probably millions more that are too small to see with telescopes.

The area in space between Jupiter and Mars where most of the asteroids are located is called the **asteroid belt**. It is 100 million miles (161 million km) wide. The illustration on pages 14 and 15 shows the position of the asteroid belt.

Not all asteroids are in the asteroid belt. One group of asteroids called the Trojans is located close to Jupiter. A few asteroids, known as the Centaurs, have been discovered close to the planet Neptune. The Amor asteroids intersect Mars's orbit, while the Apollo asteroids cross Earth's orbit.

The Atens asteroids are found inside Earth's orbit. The first Aten was discovered by astronomer Eleanor Helin in 1976. Since then, twenty-four others have been found. Because these asteroids are so close to Earth, they are a potential threat to our planet.

Asteroids have orbited the Sun along with the planets since the **solar system** formed almost 5 billion years ago. But we discovered them only 200 years ago—after the invention of the modern telescope.

This view of three asteroids was created by combining images taken by the NEAR spacecraft in 1997 and the Galileo spacecraft in 1991.

A Long Journey

It takes the average asteroid about 5 years to make one orbit around the Sun.

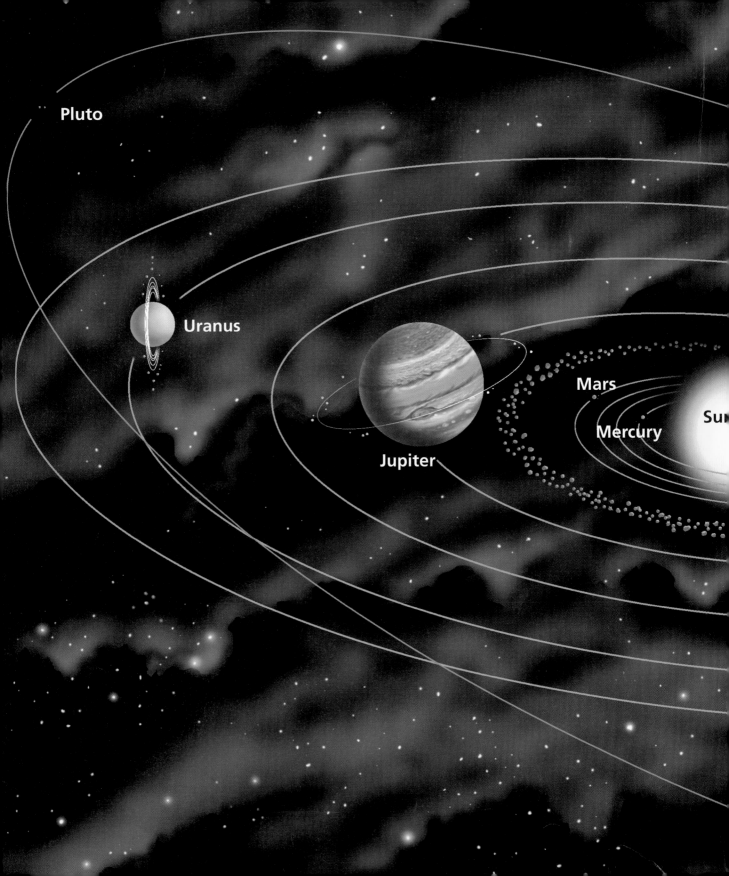

The Solar System

Venus

Moon

Earth

Asteroid Belt

Saturn

Neptune

Kirkwood Gaps

In the movie *Star Wars*, there is a scene in which Han Solo must maneuver his spaceship through an asteroid belt. Asteroids fly at him from all directions, threatening to collide with his ship. Solo narrowly escapes.

This illustration shows a small spacecraft moving through a cluster of asteroids. In reality, individual asteroids are usually million of miles apart.

In real life, traveling through the asteroid belt would not be so dangerous. For the most part, asteroids are not bunched together. Spacecraft flying through the asteroid belt have found that asteroids are separated by large empty spaces. In fact, you could be in the middle of the asteroid belt and not see even one. Sometimes they are separated by millions of miles.

Some empty regions of the asteroid belt are called Kirkwood Gaps. The asteroids that used to be in some Kirkwood Gaps flew too close to Jupiter and were pulled into the planet. Other Kirkwood Gaps exist in places where asteroids traveled so far from Jupiter that the planet lost its hold on them. Those asteroids were pulled into the inner solar system.

Space Debris

Most astronomers believe that asteroids are rocky debris left over from the formation of our solar system. Our solar system was originally a **nebula** of dust and gas in orbit around the Sun. Out of this sea of dust and gas the nine planets were born: Mercury, Venus, Earth, Mars, Jupiter, Saturn, Uranus, Neptune, and Pluto. More than sixty moons also took shape. Millions of comets and asteroids were "left over."

Four of the planets—Mercury, Venus, Earth, and Mars—are considered terrestrial or rocky. They are made mostly of rock and metal. The jovian or gas planets—Jupiter, Saturn, Uranus, and Neptune—are balls of hydrogen, helium, and other gases. Scientists aren't sure what Pluto is made of.

Scientists believe that our solar system formed from a nebula that originally looked similar to this one.

No Close Encounters

For 7 months in 1972 and 1973, the **space probe** *Pioneer 10* traveled through the asteroid belt without being hit. Later probes—*Pioneer 11*, *Voyager 1*, *Voyager 2*, and *Galileo*—also traveled safely through the belt.

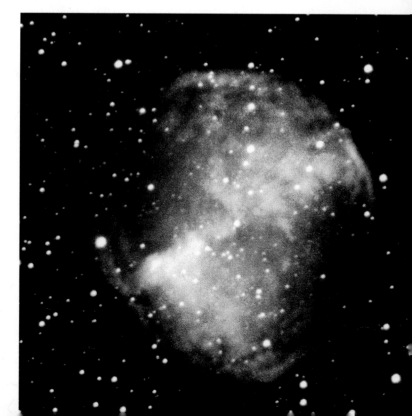

17

These views of Mars (left) and Saturn (right) show some of the differences between a terrestrial planet and a gas planet.

Asteroids as Time Capsules

Since asteroids haven't changed as much as the planets over time, they may provide clues about how the Sun and the planets formed and evolved.

The planets were formed by **gravity**. The law of gravity states that small objects are pulled toward large objects. Earth, for example, started as a ball of dust and gas. Small dust particles were drawn toward the ball, so the ball grew. As it grew larger, it attracted larger particles that eventually formed rocks. When Earth had pulled together all the space debris within its **gravitational field**, the planet was finished. This process took millions of years. The other eight planets were formed the same way, though some attracted more gas than dust.

Why weren't the asteroids pulled together into a planet? The answer lies with the biggest planet of all—Jupiter. Jupiter is about 88,840 miles (142,980 km) wide. Earth is about 7,930 miles (12,760 km) wide—more than ten times smaller. More than 1,000 planets the size of Earth could fit into Jupiter.

Because Jupiter is the largest planet in our solar system, its gravitational pull is very strong. Only the Sun has more gravitational pull than Jupiter. The asteroids are far enough away from Jupiter not to be pulled into the planet. But they are still in Jupiter's gravitational field. Jupiter pulls so strongly on the asteroids that they cannot move toward each other and form into a planet. They are destined to be "space debris" forever.

Even if all the asteroids could be brought together to form a planet, that planet would be less than half the size of the Moon. It would measure about 930 miles (1,500 km) across. The asteroid Ceres, which is 584 miles (940 km) across, would make up 25 percent of the planet.

Next in size are Pallas, Vesta, and Hygiea, which are 250 to 330 miles (400 to 530 km) across. Most asteroids are less than 200 miles (320 km) across, and many are much smaller. Only about 200 asteroids are larger than 62 miles (100 km) across.

Jupiter's tremendous gravitational force prevents the asteroids from combining into a single planet.

Mrs. Hodge points to the place where a meteorite crashed through the ceiling of her living room.

Chapter Three

Studying Asteroids on Earth

In 1954, Mrs. E. Hulitt Hodge was taking a nap on her sofa in Sylacauga, Alabama, when a 10-pound (4.5-kilogram) meteorite smashed the roof and hit her on the stomach. Luckily she had no serious injuries, just a nasty bruise.

Some meteorites, like the one that hit Mrs. Hodge, are pieces of asteroids that have fallen to Earth. The meteorite that

Meteorite Strikes Recorded in History

Year	Place	What Happened
616	China	Chariots were destroyed, and ten men were killed by meteorites.
1794	Italy	A meteorite fragment pierced a child's hat. Lucily, the child was not hurt.
1847	Bohemia	Three children were covered with debris after a 40-pound (18-kg) meteorite fell through their bedroom ceiling.
1927	Japan	A girl was bruised on the head by a tiny meteorite.
1946	Mexico	Twenty-eight people were injured and several homes were demolished by meteorites.

smacked Mrs. Hodge had traveled millions of miles before it came to an abrupt stop on her stomach.

How do asteroids or pieces of asteroids—meteoroids—get to Earth? About once every 100,000 years, two asteroids collide in space. One of them, or a piece of one, may be knocked out of the asteroid belt. It is also possible for the gravity of Earth or another planet to pull an asteroid out of the belt. When an asteroid is knocked or pulled out of its orbit, it may start moving toward the Sun.

On the way to the Sun, it will cross the orbits of Mars, Earth, Venus, and Mercury. If it gets too close to one of these planets, it may be pulled in by the planet's gravity. Once inside a planet's atmosphere, the asteroid or meteoroid rubs against all the particles that make up the atmosphere. The **friction**

5 cm

2 in.

between the space rock, which is moving at speeds of about 50,000 miles (80,500 km) per hour, and the particles in the atmosphere creates heat. You can demonstrate this principle by rubbing your palms together. Rubbing causes friction, and friction creates heat. The faster you rub your palms together, the hotter they become!

This meteorite is a fragment of the asteroid Vesta.

Friction makes the asteroid or meteoroid so hot that it begins to glow. As you learned earlier, this glow is called a meteor. Most space rocks begin to glow when they are 80 to 50 miles (130 to 80 km) above Earth. Eventually, their temperature reaches about 4,000 degrees Fahrenheit (2,050

A meteor flashes across the night sky.

degrees Celsius). Because most meteoroids are fairly small, they usually burn up before they reach Earth's surface. However, a large meteoroid may survive its trip through the atmosphere. If it does, it will crash to the planet's surface. Then it is called a meteorite.

About 200,000 meteorites strike Earth each year, but the chances of a person getting hit by a meteorite are extremely small. Only 60 people have been struck by a meteorite in the last 3,000 years. That's 1 person every 50 years. Mrs. Hodge

World-Famous Meteorites

Name	Description
Ahnighito	An explorer named Robert E. Peary discovered it in Greenland in 1895. For generations, Eskimos chipped iron off this asteroid to make knives and harpoons. It now weighs 34 tons, and is on permanent display at the Hayden Planetarium at the American Museum of Natural History in New York City.
Hoba West	Found in Namibia in southwest Africa; largest meteorite ever discovered; weighs 66 tons
Bacubirito	Discovered in Senaloa, Mexico; weighs 30 tons
Santa Catharina	Found in Brazil; weighs 25 tons

was just in the wrong place at the wrong time! Of all the people hit by meteorites, only twenty-four were killed.

The table above lists some very large meteorites that crashed into Earth. By the time most space rocks make it through the atmosphere, they are much smaller. Because they look similar to Earth rocks, most people don't even notice them.

Four stony meteorites

Most meteorites:
- are rusty brown on the outside, but some are black.
- have rounded edges because they melt as they pass through the atmosphere.
- contain some iron, so they feel heavier than many Earth rocks. Also, magnets are attracted to them.

This impressive meteorite contains rock and iron.

If you find a rock that you think might be a meteorite, try scrubbing it with an emery cloth (available at a hardware store). Polishing a stony meteorite will reveal flecks of nickel and iron. You will find a solid, bright iron and nickel interior in a metallic meteorite. If your rock is a stony-metallic meteorite, polishing will uncover flecks of olivine (olive green) crystals and sometimes large chunks of solid nickel and iron.

The American Meteorite Laboratory will test your rock for free. Send it to P.O. Box 2098, Denver, CO 80201. You could also contact the geology department of a local college or university. They may be able to test your rock for you too.

Kinds of Meteorites

There are three types of meteorites: stony, metallic, and stony-metallic. Ninety-two percent of all meteorites are made of stone. About 6 percent are made of the metals iron and nickel. The rest are made of stone, iron, and nickel. Some meteorites also contain gold, copper, platinum, iridium, and carbon.

This color-enhanced view of the asteroid Gaspra is made up of several images that were combined by a computer. The computer fit the images together in the same way that we put together a jigsaw puzzle.

Chapter Four

Studying Asteroids in Space

Scientists also learn about asteroids by observing them through telescopes. Asteroids are classified by their **brightness** and their **spectra**—the different colors of light they reflect. Scientists can get a good idea what asteroids are made of by studying their spectra and brightness.

Seventy-five percent of the asteroids we know about are very dark. They are made of stone. About 17 percent of asteroids are a little brighter. They contain two shiny metals—nickel and iron—mixed with stone and other metals. All other asteroids shine very brightly. They are made of nickel and iron.

Looking at asteroids through telescopes on Earth has also helped scientists understand how they are shaped. Most asteroids are so far away that their shape cannot be determined from only one observation. Scientists must piece together information collected by many different people.

Most large asteroids are ball-shaped. Smaller asteroids, which are usually fragments of larger asteroids, come in many different shapes. Eros is a long, skinny asteroid—22 miles (35 km) long and 10 miles (16 km) wide. Hektor looks like a dumbbell—thin in the middle and fat on both ends. Scientists have also observed asteroids shaped like potatoes, carrots, watermelons, peanut shells, and bowling pins. Some asteroids consist of two or more rocks held together by gravity.

All asteroids are scarred with **craters** that formed when they bumped into other asteroids. You can figure out an aster-

oid's age by counting its craters. The older the asteroid, the more times it has been hit and the more craters it has. When an asteroid breaks apart, the new edge of each piece will have no craters. These new, smaller asteroids are considered very "young." If an asteroid has a few craters on its new side, we know it has been around long enough to get a few hits.

You can test this idea using a large piece of white paper, a paintbrush, and several different colors of paint. Dip the paintbrush in paint, then lightly shake it over the paper. Imagine that the paint splotches are craters. Count the number of "craters" you have created. Now dip the paintbrush in a different color and shake it over the paper again. Repeat the process with a third color.

This color-enhanced view of the asteroid Ida shows its heavily cratered surface.

The older the paper (the longer you have been working on it), the more craters there will be. You also will see that most of the craters are small, and that some of the newer craters overlap or cover the older ones. This looks similar to the surface of an asteroid.

An Eye in the Sky

Scientists got their closest look at asteroids in 1991 and 1993, when the space probe *Galileo* whizzed by two asteroids on its way to the planet Jupiter.

In October 1991, *Galileo* passed within 1,000 miles (1,600 km) of the asteroid Gaspra. The pictures *Galileo* sent back to Earth showed that there are no large craters on Gaspra. According to scientists at the National Aeronautics and Space Administration's (NASA) Jet Propulsion Laboratory, ". . . this probably means that Gaspra is relatively young, and simply hasn't picked up any major scars as yet."

Galileo made a startling discovery when it flew past the asteroid Ida in August 1993. Ida has a moon. Scientists named the moon Dactyl. Now scientists think many asteroids may have moons.

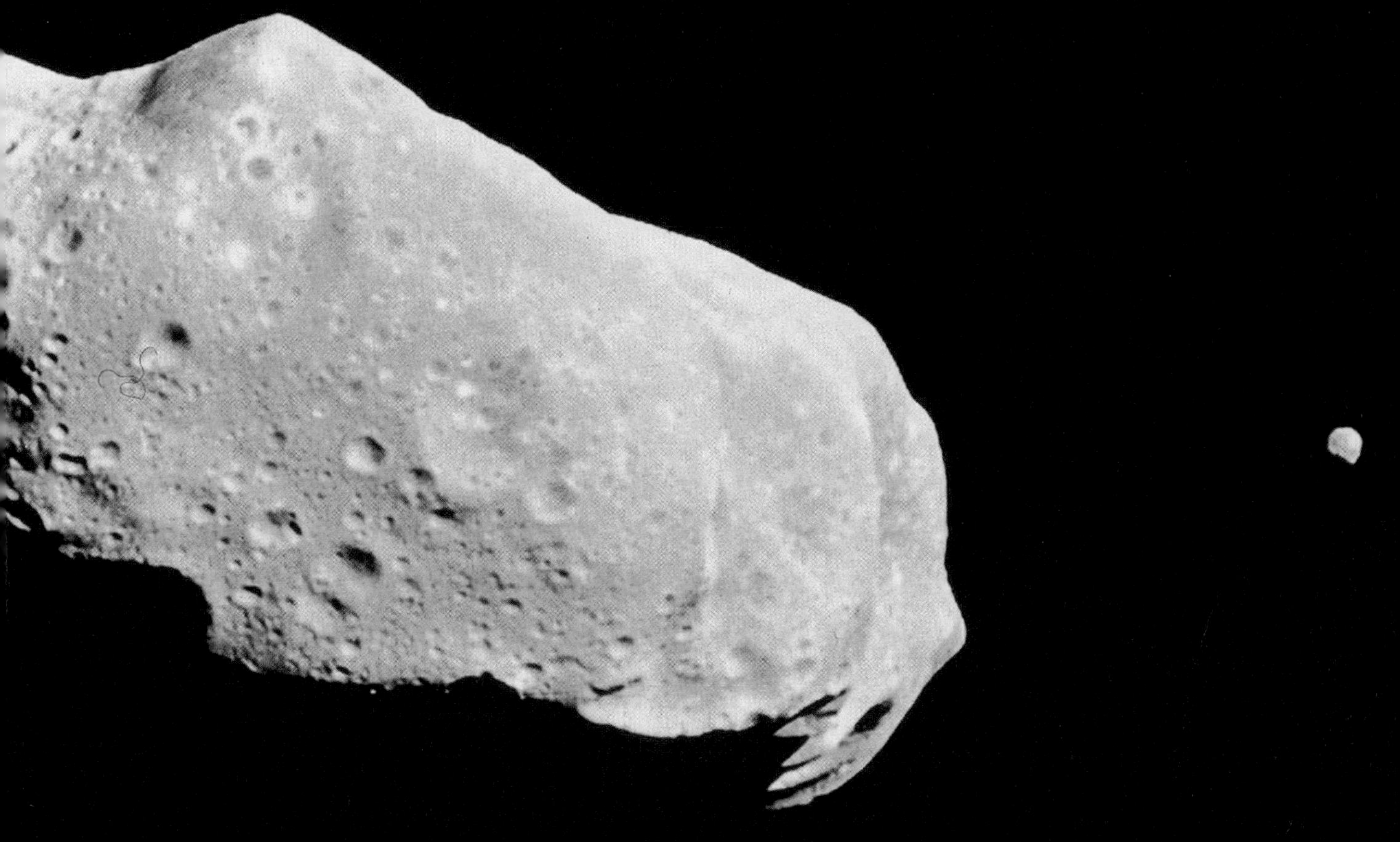

Images taken by Galileo *showed scientists on Earth that Ida has its own moon.*

Barringer Meteor Crater
in Arizona

Chapter Five

Hits and Misses

Early in Earth's history, asteroids bombarded the planet regularly. We know this from huge impact craters found all over the world. More than 150 craters have been found. Many more—perhaps 1,000—are not visible from the ground. They are either too large, underwater, buried, or eroded and overgrown.

Barringer Meteor Crater in Arizona was the first impact crater to be discovered. Found in 1920, it is about 4,000 feet (1,200 m) wide and 49,000 years old. Scientists believe it was created by an asteroid about 40 feet (12 m) wide.

Chicxulub on Mexico's Yucatan Peninsula is probably the most famous impact crater in the world. As you learned earlier, scientists think this crater was created by an asteroid that hit Earth 65 million years ago. This asteroid was probably responsible for the death of most life on Earth, including the dinosaurs.

Famous Craters

Name	Location	Description
Canyon Diablo	Arizona	Contains many meteorites weighing 20 to 2,000 tons
Everglades National Park	Near Miami, Florida	Some scientists believe this 5,000-square-mile (12,900-sq-km) subtropical swamp is actually an impact crater.
Kara Kul	Pamir Mountain Range near Afghanistan	28 miles (45 km) wide; filled with water
Lake Manicouagan	Quebec, Canada	44 miles (70 km) wide; inside a 60-mile (96-km)-wide crater
Ries Basin	Southern Germany	17 miles (27 km) wide
Unnamed	Kentland, Indiana	8 miles (13 km) wide
Unnamed	Near Manson, Iowa	25 miles (40 km) wide; hidden under cornfields
Vredefort Dome	South Africa	87 miles (140 km) wide

Other craters ranging from 2,500 feet (760 m) to about 200 miles (320 km) across have been found in Africa, North and South America, Australia, Canada, Europe, and the Middle East. Most of the impacts that caused these craters occurred thousands—if not millions—of years ago. But asteroid hits are not just a thing of the past. In fact, an asteroid 200 feet (60 m) wide almost hit Earth less than 100 years ago.

Some people claim that Gasses Bluff is the most beautiful meteorite impact crater on Earth.

The Tunguska Event

Few people saw the huge fireball that blazed across the sky near the Tunguska region of Russia on the morning of June 30, 1908. But people heard the explosion as far as 600 miles (970 km) away. The force of the explosion was so powerful that earthquake-detecting instruments in England—3,400 miles (5,500 km) away—picked it up. The jolt uprooted, flattened, and burned trees for 2,000 square miles (5,200 sq km)—an area nearly as big as Delaware—and killed herds of reindeer.

This Russian forest was knocked down by the tremendous force of the Tunguska event.

What caused the massive explosion? Because it occurred in such a desolate area, scientists weren't able to visit the site until 1937. At that time, they found no evidence of a meteorite, a volcanic explosion, a bomb, or an earthquake. For many years, the most popular theory was that an alien spaceship had exploded in the air, though many scientists believed an exploding comet might have caused the blast.

In 1996, a team of Italian scientists revisited the explosion site. Using modern equipment, they found tiny particles of copper, gold, and nickel embedded in trees. They concluded that these minerals probably came from an asteroid. Scientists estimate that the Tunguska asteroid was 200 feet (60 m) wide and entered Earth's atmosphere traveling 50,000 miles (80,500 km) per hour. The asteroid didn't hit Earth—friction and air pressure caused it to blow up about 4 miles (6.4 km) above the ground. The force of the mid-air explosion equaled 10 to 20 million tons of dynamite.

If the object that caused the damage at Tunguska was indeed an asteroid, it was the first asteroid to damage Earth in recorded human history. If it had exploded over Moscow, just 2,300 miles (3,700 km) to the west, tens of thousands of people would have died.

Earth-Crossing Asteroids

A Tunguska-sized asteroid enters Earth's atmosphere about once a century. But because 75 percent of Earth is covered with water, most of these asteroids explode over the ocean.

You Oughta Be in Pictures

Two Hollywood block-busters, *Deep Impact* and *Armageddon*, came out in the summer of 1998. They cashed in on people's fears of an asteroid or comet colliding with Earth.

Just such an explosion occurred over the South Atlantic Ocean in the late 1960s.

Scientists estimate that about 1,700 asteroids larger than 2,500 feet (760 m) wide cross Earth's path as it orbits the Sun. If an asteroid that big hit Earth, it would cause worldwide damage. The impact would send a huge dust cloud into the air, blocking the Sun's light and warmth. Without sunlight, crops would fail all over the world. People and animals would starve. Billions of people could die.

"It's something like a one in a million chance in any given year that one of those impacts would take place," says David Morrison, chief of the Space Science Department at NASA's

This illustration shows a group of asteroids approaching Earth. Is our planet in danger?

Ames Research Center in California. The chances of a collision within the next century are small—about 1 in 1,000.

The chance of a smaller asteroid hitting Earth in any given year is about 1 in 300,000. A smaller asteroid could cause significant damage and kill thousands of people, but it would not have lasting global effects.

An asteroid larger than 1 mile (1.6 km) in diameter hits Earth about once in a million years. An asteroid larger than 5 miles (8 km) wide strikes about once every 10 million years.

Some 150 Earth-crossing asteroids have been located. A few of them are described in the table below. Others include Icarus, Aten, Phaeton, 1996 JA1, and 1996 JG. No asteroid is known to be on a collision course with Earth right now, but that could change at any time.

Some Earth-Crossing Asteroids

Name	Description
Hermes	3,500 feet (1,066 m) wide; in 1937, missed Earth by 485,000 miles (780,500 km)—about twice the distance between Earth and the Moon
Geographos	2.5 miles (4 km) long and 2,500 feet (760 m) wide; passed within 5.6 million miles (9 million km) of Earth in 1969
4581 Asclepius	2,500 feet (760 m) wide; passed within 450,000 miles (724,000 km) of Earth in 1989; will make another close fly-by in 2015
Sisyphus	About 6 miles (10 km) wide; discovered in 1992
Hephaistos	About 6 miles (10 km) wide; discovered in 1992

Scientists estimate that the risk of being killed by a tornado is about the same as the risk of dying from an asteroid impact.

Chapter Six

Guarding The Planet

The risk of dying from an asteroid impact is about the same as the risk of dying from a hurricane, tornado, earthquake, or flood. Each person has a 1 in 20,000 chance each year of dying from one of these natural disasters.

But the difference between asteroids and other natural disasters, as NASA's David Morrison told the U.S. Congress in 1993, is that "cosmic impacts can be avoided. We have the means to protect our planet if we choose to do so."

In 1991, the U.S. government started taking the threat of asteroid impacts seriously. That year, the Committee on Science and Technology of the U.S. House of Representatives released the following statement:

> The chances of the Earth being struck by a large asteroid are extremely small, but since the consequences of such a collision are extremely large, the Committee believes it is only prudent to assess the nature of the threat and prepare to deal with it.

In 1992, the Committee asked NASA for help. A group of NASA scientists wrote a paper called *The Spaceguard Survey Report*. The report recommended using a network of telescopes located all over the world to search for Earth-crossing asteroids measuring at least 2,500 feet (760 m) across.

Asteroid Panic

On March 11, 1998, Asteroid 1997XF11 made front-page news. It was reported that the space rock was on a collision course with Earth and could hit the planet in October 2028.

While scientists discussed what could be done to avoid the disaster, some people panicked. But the report turned out to be wrong. The next day, scientists told the public that they had done more mathematical calculations and were sure there was no chance Earth was in the asteroid's path.

As a result of this unnecessary scare, NASA asked scientists not to release news of any Earth-threatening asteroid or comet without watching it for at least 72 hours.

Programs to Detect Asteroids

Congress has not decided yet whether to fund the Spaceguard Survey, but it currently supports some other asteroid search programs. Most of the money goes to three programs:

Dr. Tom Gehrels is now searching for near-Earth asteroids. Before that, he was involved in an experiment conducted by Pioneer 10. Here, he poses with results from that experiment.

- Dr. Tom Gehrels of the University of Arizona is searching for near-Earth asteroids from Kitt Peak, Arizona. His project, called Spacewatch, discovers about three near-Earth asteroids each month. The computer-controlled telescope, which is programmed to detect moving objects, scans the sky on 18 nights each month. Soon, a second telescope will work from a site in India. If a third telescope was set up in the Far East, it would be possible to cover almost all of the sky.

- Since 1995, Eleanor Helin and her colleagues at the NASA/Caltech Jet Propulsion Lab have been working on the Near-Earth Asteroid Tracking (NEAT) program with the U.S. Air Force. NEAT's computer-controlled telescope is located on top of Mount Haleakala on the island of Maui in Hawaii. It searches the sky on 6 nights each month. By May 1997, the telescope had detected more than 10,000 space objects. Fifty percent of these objects had never been seen before. It found 700 asteroids in January 1997 alone.

- Ted Bowell is creating a new search camera for the Lowell Observatory's Near-Earth Object Survey (LONEOS) in Flagstaff, Arizona.

Other countries are concerned about asteroids too. Since March 1997, the Spaceguard Foundation in Italy has been promoting and coordinating a program to locate asteroids that may cross Earth's orbit. Their plan calls for a half-dozen computer-controlled telescopes around the world. Russia, Japan, and China have programs in place, too.

Preventing an Asteroid Impact

In the last few years, scientists and weapons experts from all over the world have met six times to discuss possible ways to defend our planet against asteroids. NASA's David Morrison attended these meetings and headed the group of scientists who wrote *The Spaceguard Survey Report*. According to him, there are two ways to deal with an aster-oid heading toward Earth: "One is give it a shove. The other is just try to break it up into little pieces so when they hit, they don't do as much damage."

If an asteroid is on a course to hit Earth in a few years, crashing a rocket into it could nudge the space rock out of Earth's path. However, if an asteroid could hit Earth within a few months, a more powerful shove would be needed. In that case, a powerful rocket could carry a nuclear bomb into space. The nuclear bomb would be designed to explode when the rocket got close to the asteroid. If all went well, the force of the explosion would push the asteroid off its collision course with Earth.

David Morrison is the chief of the Space Science Department at NASA's Ames Research Center in California.

However, there are several reasons why this method might not work. Some asteroids are not one solid rock. They are piles of rubble held together by gravity. If a nuclear bomb exploded near such an asteroid, most of the bomb's energy would be absorbed by the empty spaces between the fragments and the asteroid would not move.

Trying to blow up an asteroid is even riskier. If the asteroid does not break up into pieces small enough to burn up in Earth's atmosphere, the large pieces might cause even more

A Space Shield

At a 1996 meeting, a Russian scientist named A.V. Zaitzov revealed that his country is developing a Space Shield defense system. The system is based on a rocket called Zenit that can be readied for launch in 90 minutes. Zaitsov's idea is to play "cosmic billiards" by using one nonthreatening asteroid to knock a threatening one out of Earth's orbit. The Zenit rocket would crash into the nonthreatening asteroid and set it on a path toward the dangerous one. The collision would hopefully destroy both asteroids.

During World War II, Edward Teller came up with the design for the hydrogen bomb. More recently, he has suggested a scheme for protecting Earth from asteroids.

damage than the original asteroid would have. That's why this method would only be used if the asteroid is decades away from hitting Earth.

Scientist Edward Teller, who came up with the design for the hydrogen bomb, thinks there is a way to stop small asteroids without using nuclear weapons. He has suggested using a three-dimensional net consisting of millions of **tungsten** "bullets." The heavy net would be carried into space by a rocket. When an asteroid less than 600 feet (180 m) wide passes through the net, the space rock would be torn into tiny pieces.

In March 1993, while Congress was discussing the threat of asteroids, Representative George E. Brown Jr. stated:

> If some day in the future we discover well in advance that an asteroid that is big enough to cause a mass extinction is going to hit the Earth, and then we alter the course of that asteroid so that it does not hit us, it will be one of the most important accomplishments in all of human history.

According to a report written by the American Institute of Aeronautics and Astronautics (AIAA) in 1995, the opposite is also true. If an asteroid strikes Earth and wipes out the human race and millions of other species, and we could have prevented it, but didn't, it would be a crime. The people who wrote the paper believe that we humans have a responsibility to protect ourselves, other living creatures, and our planet from harm.

An artist's representation of the asteroid Eros approaching Earth

Chapter Seven

Going the Distance

Right now, the 22-mile (35-km) asteroid known as 433 Eros is orbiting Earth. It does not cross Earth's orbit—yet. But scientists at the University of Pisa in Italy have been watching it closely. They say that eventually, Earth will be directly in Eros's path.

Eros is the largest asteroid near Earth. It is twice as big as the asteroid that wiped out the dinosaurs. If it smashes into Earth, all living things could die. Scientists know that the best way to

An artist's representation of NEAR orbiting Eros

prevent this destruction is to learn as much as possible about the asteroid.

In February 1998, NASA launched the Near Earth Asteroid Rendezvous (NEAR) spacecraft. It flew by Eros in December 1998 and will begin to orbit and study the asteroid in May 2000. At times, NEAR will be just 15 miles (24 km) from Eros.

NEAR will study Eros's size and weight, find out what it is made of, and study its gravitational and **magnetic fields**. The spacecraft will map Eros's entire surface and take lots of pictures. The mission will give us our closest look yet at an asteroid. If there is enough fuel left at the end of the mission, scientists will let NEAR slowly crash into the asteroid, so the spacecraft can take super-up-close pictures.

If we have the technology to crash a piece of equipment from Earth into an asteroid, surely we can develop a way stop an asteroid from smashing into us! There is no need for humankind to experience a nightmarish catastrophe like the one that ended the reign of the dinosaurs.

Glossary

asteroid—a piece of rocky debris left over from the formation of the solar system 4.6 billion years ago. Most asteroids orbit the Sun in a belt between Mars and Jupiter.

asteroid belt—the region in space between Mars and Jupiter where most asteroids are found. It is 100 million miles (161 million km) wide.

atmosphere—the gases that surround a planet or other body in space.

brightness—the amount of light given off or reflected by an object.

comet—a small ball of rock and ice that orbits the Sun. When it gets close to the Sun, some of the ice melts and releases gases. These gases form a tail behind the comet.

crater—an irregular circular or oval hole made by a collision with another object.

evolve—to change over time. Living things evolve by developing traits that help them survive in their environment.

friction—a force that resists the motion between two objects or surfaces. If there is motion, energy is converted to heat.

gravitational field—the area of space affected by a planet's gravity.

gravity—the force that pulls objects toward the center of a planet or other body in space.

iridium—a rare metal similar to gold.

magnetic field—the area surrounding a planet in which magnetic force is felt.

mammal—an animal that has a backbone and feeds its young with mother's milk.

meteor—the glowing light we see in the night sky when a meteoroid is in contact with Earth's atmosphere.

meteorite—a particle of dust or rock that hits the surface of another object, such as a moon or planet.

meteoroid—a rocky or metallic object of relatively small size, usually once part of a comet or asteroid.

nebula—a giant cloud of gas and dust in space. Our solar system formed from a nebula.

orbit—the curved path followed by one body going around another body in space.

reptile—an animal that lives on land, lays eggs, and is cold-blooded. Examples include alligators, turtles, snakes, and lizards.

solar system—the Sun and all the objects—planets, moons, asteroids, and comets—that orbit it.

space probe—an unmanned spacecraft carrying scientific instruments that orbits the Sun on its way to one or more planets. It may fly past a planet it has been aimed at, orbit the planet, or, in some cases, even land there.

spectra—the pattern (set of colors) of light waves reflected by an asteroid.

tungsten—a very hard metal.

To Find
Out More

Books

Branley, Franklin M. *Comets, Meteoroids, and Asteroids*. New York: Crowell, 1974.

Heathcote, Nick. *The New Discovery Book of Space*. New York: New Discovery Books, 1994.

Kraske, Robert. *Asteroids: Invaders from Space*. New York: Atheneum Books for Young Readers, 1995.

Simon, Seymour. *Comets, Meteors, and Asteroids*. New York: Morrow Junior Books,1994.

Sipiera, Paul. *The Solar System*. Danbury, CT: Children's Press, 1997.

Stoot, Carole. *Night Sky*. New York: Dorling Kindersley, 1993.

Verdet, Jean-Pierre. *Earth, Sky, and Beyond: A Journey Through Space*. New York: Lodestar, 1995.

Online Sites

Asteroid and Comet Impact Hazards
http://impact.arc.nasa.gov/index.html
Has up-to-date information on the status of the Spaceguard Survey, copies of papers submitted by NASA and AIAA, responses from members of Congress, and descriptions of programs that search for asteroids and comets.

Closest Approaches to the Earth by Minor Planets
http://cfa-www.harvard.edu/cfa/ps/lists/Closest.html
Lists the asteroids closest to Earth.

NASA's Quest Project
http://quest.arc.nasa.gov
A list and description of educational programs.

The Near Earth Asteroid Tracking Home Page
http://huey.jpl.nasa.gov/~spravdo/neat.html
Includes general information about the NEAT program and *Deep Space 1*, images of asteroids, and more.

Places To Visit

These museums and science centers are great places to learn more about asteroids and the solar system.

Flandrau Science Center and Planetarium
University of Arizona
Tucson, AZ 85721

Hansen Planetarium
15 South State Street
Salt Lake City, UT 84111

Hayden Planetarium
American Museum of Natural History
Central Park West at 79th St.
New York, NY 10024

Howell Observatory
1400 W. Mars Hill Rd.
Flagstaff, AZ 86001

Miami Museum of Science and Space Transit Planetarium
3280 South Miami Avenue
Miami, FL 33129

The Newark Museum and Dreyfus Planetarium
49 Washington Street
P.O. Box 540
Newark, NJ 07101-0540

Reuben H. Fleet Space Theater and Science Center
1875 El Prado Way
P.O. Box 33303
San Diego, CA 92163-3303

Schiele Museum of Natural History and Planetarium, Inc.
1500 East Garrison Blvd.
Gastonia, NC 28054

Space Center
Top of New Mexico Highway 2001
P.O. Box 533
Alamogordo, NM 88311-0533

Space Center Houston
1601 NASA Road One
Houston, TX 77058

A Note on Sources

When researching this book, I found that basic facts about asteroids and other space topics are well covered in a variety of books, but these "facts" must be checked carefully. One of the most exciting things about space science is that new discoveries are made every day.

To make sure that the most up-to-date information is included in this book, I read many newspaper and magazine articles. These provide in-depth information about fairly recent discoveries.

The most current sources of information about space science are Internet websites. I chose sites developed and maintained by either colleges and universities with respected space science programs or professional organizations, such as the National Aeronautics and Space Administration (NASA) and the Jet Propulsion Laboratory (JPL). New information is constantly being added to these sites.

—*Samantha Bonar*

Index

Numbers in *italics* indicate illustrations.

About the Author

Samantha Bonar is an editor at the *Los Angeles Times* and a freelance writer. She is the author of *Comets*, which was published by Franklin Watts in 1998. She has also written numerous magazine articles for *American Girl*, *Boys' Life*, *Highlights*, *National Geographic World*, *Owl (Canada)*, *Ranger Rick*, *Contact Kids*, and many other publications. Ms. Bonar lives in Altadena, California.